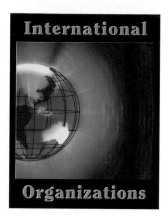

International

Organizations

Amnesty International

Deena Banks

WORLD ALMANAC® LIBRARY

Please visit our web site at: www.worldalmanaclibrary.com
For a free color catalog describing World Almanac® Library's list
of high-quality books and multimedia programs, call 1-800-848-2928 (USA)
or 1-800-387-3178 (Canada). World Almanac® Library's fax: (414) 332-3567.

Library of Congress Cataloging-in-Publication Data

Banks, Deena.
    Amnesty International / by Deena Banks.
        p. cm. — (International organizations)
    Includes bibliographical references and index.
    Contents: Human rights: a vision — The setting of goals — Working for human rights —
Campaigns and urgent actions — Success stories.
    ISBN 0-8368-5517-5 (lib. bdg.)
    ISBN 0-8368-5526-4 (softcover)
    1. Amnesty International—Juvenile literature. 2. Human rights—Juvenile literature.
[1. Amnesty International. 2. Human rights.] I. Title. II. International organizations
(Milwaukee, Wis.)
JC571.B343   2003
323'.06'01—dc21   2003045030

First published in 2004 by
World Almanac® Library
330 West Olive Street, Suite 100
Milwaukee, WI 53212 USA

Developed by Books Two, Inc.
Editor: Jean B. Black
Design and Maps: Krueger Graphics, Inc.: Karla J. Krueger and Victoria L. Buck
Indexer: Chandelle Black
World Almanac® Library editor: JoAnn Early Macken
World Almanac® Library art direction: Tammy Gruenewald

Logo © Amnesty International Publications. http://www.amnesty.org.
Photo Credits: Amnesty International Photos: 22, 25, 26, 31, 33, 41; © AP Photo: 5; © AP
Photo/Daily Progress Leslie Close: 14; © AP Photo/Itsuo Inouye: 16; © AP Photo/John Redman:
24; © AP Photo/Maxim Marmur: 21; © AP Photo/MTI, Imre Foeldi: 7; © AP Photo/POOL 29;
© AP Photo/Scott Dalton: 13; © AP Photo/Wally Santana: 36; Courtesy of IREX: 11;
© Macduff Everton/CORBIS: 35; Reuters/Bobby Yip: cover; Reuters/Ian Hodgson: 43;
© Scott Langley/LangleyCreations.com: 38; United Nations Photo Library: 8, 19, 28, 30;
© WITNESS/CORBIS SYGMA: 17

Printed in the United States of America

1 2 3 4 5 6 7 8 9 07 06 05 04 03

TABLE OF CONTENTS

Words that appear in the glossary are printed in
boldface type the first time they occur in the text.

Human Rights: A Vision

In a small village where secrets are difficult to keep, a young woman hoped only to be left in peace. She cradled her newborn daughter tenderly. With no husband, she would have to raise the infant alone.

Unfortunately, local police came to arrest her. She was put on trial, even though she had no lawyer. On March 22, 2002, the court found Amina Lawal, who was thirty years old, guilty. What was her crime? She was an unmarried woman who became pregnant. How would she be punished? She would be stoned to death.

Amina lived in a village in northern Nigeria, a country that has more people than any other African country. Strict religious laws had recently been passed in Katsina State, where Amina lived. These laws made many actions crimes, and some of these crimes could be punished by the death penalty. A person could be put to death by stoning, beheading, or other means.

Stoning was especially cruel. It required the men in Amina's village to bury her in sand up to her neck and then throw stones at her head. It would probably take her many hours to die.

The village was all that Amina knew. The youngest of thirteen children in a Muslim family, she never learned to read or write. She was married at the age of fourteen. Her husband later divorced her, and she was left to raise two children on her own. Another marriage also ended in divorce.

Sixteen months after the second divorce, Amina had a baby girl, Wasila. The man she identified as Wasila's father said the baby was not his. The matter was brought into court. The court said four male witnesses were needed to prove he was the father, but no witnesses showed up. The court said there was no evidence and allowed the man she identified as the father to go. Meanwhile, Amina was put in jail.

Would no one stand up for her?

Fortunately, some **women's-rights** groups heard about the case. They hired a lawyer for Amina. The lawyer and her team started a series of appeals. An appeal is a legal process of moving a case to a higher court in the hope of getting a different decision. Amina's lawyer wanted a court to reverse her death sentence.

Soon, Amina's story came to the attention of a group called Amnesty International. One of Amnesty International's most important jobs is to defend people who cannot defend themselves. This means working on behalf of individuals and against unjust courts, govern-ments, and others in power. Even though Amina now had a lawyer, more help was needed.

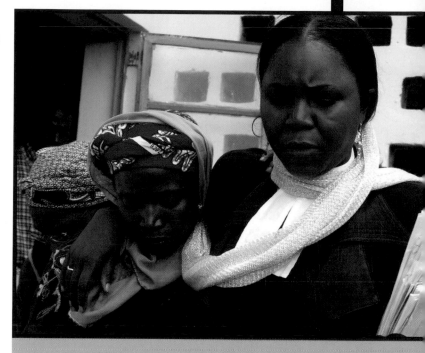

Amina Lawal (left) walked with her attorney in 2002 after her death sentence for having a child out of marriage was confirmed by one appeals court.

Three months after announcing the death sentence, the judge reviewed his decision. He ruled that Amina's execution could wait until January 2004. This would allow her to finish nursing her baby. But she would still have to be put to death.

Further appeals did not go well. Two more courts supported the original sentence. It did not matter that Amina had become pregnant before the new laws were passed.

As the appeals continued, government officials admitted that the death penalty violated the Nigerian constitution. It also went against agreements Nigeria had signed with other countries to ban cruel punish-ments. However, authorities did nothing to overturn the death sentence.

Meanwhile, Amnesty International made Amina's story front-page news. Volunteers in many countries organized events to educate the general public. They urged people to send letters, faxes, and **petitions** to the Nigerian government. The petitions asked for Amina to be pardoned and freed. In England, organizers presented Nigerian officials with more than one million signatures.

In the United States, TV star Oprah Winfrey told viewers about Amina. She put a letter on her web site that people could e-mail to Nigerian authorities. The U.S. government even got involved. Congress introduced a resolution to condemn death by stoning. It also criticized other abuses of women's rights in Nigeria.

International pressure built. A "Miss World" beauty contest had been scheduled to take place in Nigeria. Several countries pulled their contestants out of it in protest over Amina's death sentence. Eventually, the contest was moved elsewhere because of rioting sparked by a newspaper article about the pageant that offended Muslims.

In just a few short months, hundreds of thousands of people had joined the fight to save Amina Lawal's life. Several layers of appeals are expected before her case reaches Nigeria's Supreme Court.

What is Amnesty International?

Amnesty International, or AI, is an organization dedicated to protecting human rights all over the world. It was formed in 1961 and has since grown to 1.7 million members in more than 160 countries. Members from all walks of life volunteer their time, money, and energy. They often work with others in their communities, such as people in youth or church groups. The groups sometimes join with others

Vision of Amnesty International

Amnesty International's vision is one of a world in which every person enjoys all the human rights enshrined in the Universal Declaration of Human Rights (see pages 8 and 9) and other international human-rights standards.

to form larger networks that give people from different cities or countries opportunities to work together toward common goals.

Amnesty International is independent—it does not receive money from governments or political officials. Instead, volunteer groups and networks raise money from the public. This allows Amnesty International to freely continue its work.

Furthermore, Amnesty International is impartial—it does not favor one government or political party over any other. Nor does it favor one religion or set of beliefs over any other, including those of the people it protects. It does not answer to the U.S., British, Chinese, or any other government. It answers only to people it tries to protect.

Amnesty International works primarily by calling attention to human-rights violations. These Hungarian human-rights activists protested domestic violence against Russian women on International Women's Day in 2003. The sign says, "364 days of violence, one day of flowers. Are you kidding?!"

Because so many people regularly fall victim to human-rights abuses throughout the world, Amnesty International must look everywhere. It cannot single out just one region, country, or government to examine. In 2002, it defended citizens against the governments of countries ranging from Australia to Zimbabwe and from Iraq to the United States. No

Eleanor Roosevelt, a great advocate of human rights, showed a poster of the newly adopted Universal Declaration of Human Rights in 1948.

country is above the law. Amnesty International's philosophy is that all nations should respect the human rights of those within their borders—citizens and visitors alike.

Human Rights

When people are born, they have certain rights just because they are human beings. For example, every person is born free. Humans cannot be bought, sold, or owned by others. Everyone has human rights regardless of their race, sex, religion, birthplace, culture, or beliefs. Human rights do not have to be earned. Nor can they be taken away, by the government or anyone else. If a person's human rights are violated—for example, if he or she is put in jail without a fair trial—the authorities who do so must be held accountable.

Amnesty International recognizes many human rights to which

Universal Declaration of Human Rights

This Declaration was adopted by the United Nations General Assembly on December 10, 1948. It forms the basis of international human-rights law, and many nations have agreed to honor it. However, worldwide abuse of human rights continues. As we enter the twenty-first century, Amnesty International continues working to ensure that all people enjoy the human rights to which they are entitled. Thirty sections, or Articles, of the Declaration describe specific human rights. They are summarized here.

Article 1: All human beings are free and equal in dignity and rights.

Article 2: Everyone is entitled to human rights regardless of their race, color, sex, language, religion, politics, class, or birthplace.

Article 3: Everyone has the right to life, liberty, and security of person.

Article 4: No one shall be held in slavery or servitude.

Article 5: No one shall suffer from torture or from cruel, inhuman, or degrading treatment.

Article 6: All people shall be treated equally by the law.

Article 7: All people are entitled to equal protection by the law and shall not be discriminated against.

Article 8: All people have the right to an effective remedy by the law.

Article 9: No one shall be arrested, detained, or exiled without reason.

Article 10: Everyone has the right to a fair and public hearing by an independent court.

Article 11: All persons charged with an offense are presumed innocent until proven guilty at a public trial.

Article 12: Everyone has the right to privacy of family, home, and correspondence without interference.

Article 13: Everyone has the right to freedom of movement and residence in their own country as well as the right to leave, go, or return to other countries.

Article 14: Everyone has the right to political **asylum** in other countries.

Article 15: Everyone has the right to a nationality.

Article 16: Everyone has the right to marry and have a family, and men and women are entitled to equal rights in marriage.

Article 17: Everyone has the right to own property.

Article 18: Everyone has freedom of thought, conscience, and religion.

Article 19: Everyone has freedom of opinion and expression.

Article 20: Everyone has freedom of association and peaceful assembly.

Article 21: Everyone has the right to take part in and select government.

Article 22: Everyone has the right to social security and all economic, social, and cultural rights necessary for their dignity and development.

Article 23: Everyone has the right to work, freely choose their work, and receive equal pay for equal work.

Article 24: Everyone has the right to work under reasonable conditions, receive just pay and paid holidays, and form and join trade unions.

Article 25: Everyone has the right to an adequate living standard for themselves and their families, including food, housing, clothing, medical care, and social security.

Article 26: Everyone has the right to education.

Article 27: Everyone has the right to intellectual property and participation in the cultural life of the community.

Article 28: Everyone is entitled to a social and international order that protects the rights and freedoms in this Declaration.

Article 29: Everyone has duties to the community so that all people may equally exercise these rights and freedoms.

Article 30: No person or group is allowed to do anything contrary to or destructive of these human rights and freedoms.

people are entitled. These are described in an important document, the Universal Declaration of Human Rights. The General Assembly of the United Nations adopted it in December 1948.

The Declaration is the basis of international human-rights law. It includes thirty Articles, or specific rights. Many of these relate directly to Amnesty International's activities. For example, Article 1 says that all people are born free and equal in dignity and rights. Article 5 says that no one shall suffer from torture or other cruel treatment. Article 18 says that all people have the right to form their own opinions, choose their own religions, and follow their own consciences.

Prisoners of Conscience

One of Amnesty International's most important contributions has been to identify people who are unfairly jailed. Known as prisoners of conscience, these people did not commit violent crimes such as robbery, murder, or rape. Instead, they were arrested for unfair or questionable reasons. Perhaps they belonged to an ethnic or religious minority. Perhaps they did not have the same political beliefs as those in power. Perhaps they were simply in the wrong place at the wrong time. For whatever reason, prisoners of conscience need to be recognized and protected. Otherwise, they might be forgotten.

Amnesty International's name indicates the importance of these people. "Amnesty" is the granting of a pardon, usually to a large group of people, by those who charged them in the first place. The people who are pardoned are no longer vulnerable to arrest. Amnesty International tries to gain amnesty for all prisoners of conscience.

"When a person lives in a country where he gets only little information about the outside world, he feels small, powerless and utterly defenseless against the apparatus of the dictatorship. But then if one learns that there is an organization like Amnesty—an organization which is not indifferent to the fate of those people—it gives you new strength."

— Faraj Sarkhouhi, Iran, former prisoner of conscience

The Setting of Goals

Amnesty International's basic goal is to end human-rights violations and prevent them from ever happening again. Over the years, it has found many issues that need attention. The top goals in its 2002 Annual Report included the following issues:

- freedom for prisoners of conscience
- fair and prompt trials for political prisoners
- an end to the death penalty, torture, and other cruel treatment
- an end to political killings and "disappearances"
- an end to other serious abuses of human rights (for example, **hostage** taking and racial **discrimination**)

To meet these goals, Amnesty International runs a number of campaigns. These campaigns are broad efforts organized around a theme to achieve a certain goal. Volunteer networks carry these efforts out in many countries. Often the campaigns focus on certain groups of people who suffer abuse just because of who they are. The struggle for women's rights is one example of such a campaign. Women around the globe are targets of domestic violence. In some countries they do not have the same freedoms or rights as men do. Consider Amina Lawal's case in Nigeria. The same types of law that made her a criminal for having her baby also have made it illegal for women to hold many types of jobs.

Another campaign seeks to prevent "disappearances." These are secret arrests or killings of people by police, soldiers, or others in charge. The authorities give no explanations to the victims' families. They do not even

A boy in Belarus holds up a picture of his "disappeared" father to passing crowds in Minsk, hoping someone has seen him. Several opposition leaders have disappeared since 1999.

admit knowing where the missing person is. It can take years before family members are reunited—if it ever happens.

These campaigns are just two examples of the work to be done. Amnesty International says it has saved more than forty thousand lives so far. Still, it has a long way to go. Its ultimate goal is to bring about a world where people live in freedom, peace, and dignity. In such a perfect world, a human-rights organization like Amnesty International would no longer be needed.

Abuses in Guatemala

Just to the south of Mexico lies the Central American country of Guatemala. More than thirty years of civil war have taken their toll on the citizens. **Indigenous,** or native, people have been especially hard hit. The civil war ended in 1996, but indigenous groups such as the Mayan Indians continue to suffer from racial discrimination and other abuses.

Mayans have endured discrimination ever since Europeans colonized the New World five hundred years ago. In the 1960s, fighting broke out between the military government and the citizens who opposed it. The government army killed thousands of people, trying to get rid of the opposition, but rebel bases kept springing up.

In the late 1970s, the government went after suspected rebel camps in the highlands of Guatemala. Unfortunately, many Mayans lived in these danger zones. The Guatemalan president was an army general. He ordered his troops to use a "scorched earth" policy of total destruction. The soldiers went from village to village, sparing no one. They tortured and killed men, women, and children. Then they burned everything to the ground. Several hundred Mayan villages were destroyed.

The Mayan culture—its customs and ways of life—suffered as well. For example, Mayan clothing traditionally reflected a person's village or region. But when Mayans learned their clothes linked them to certain target areas, they had to disguise themselves. They did not want government soldiers to shoot them on sight. Even after many fled to the cities, they had to keep hiding their true identities.

The final losses were high. Roughly forty-five thousand Guatemalans "disappeared." More than two hundred thousand were killed, mostly indigenous people. Human-rights observers say this amounts to **genocide**, the deliberate destruction of a racial or cultural group.

Mayans in the small Guatemalan village of Xecoxol mourn during a 1999 funeral for the reburial of relatives who had been killed years earlier. Thousands of Mayans were killed during the thirty-six-year civil war.

In the years since fighting ended, Amnesty International has investigated some of the war crimes. It has tried to bring army officials to trial, but progress is slow. A pattern of **impunity**, or freedom from punishment, seems to shield the accused.

Judges are reluctant to try cases against former officials, perhaps as the result of threats or bribes. Important evidence often is lost. Mayans and other indigenous witnesses, who may not speak Spanish, have difficulty understanding what is said in court. Some cases drag on for years. Key witnesses are often **intimidated**, and some mysteriously disappear.

Those who try to defend indigenous people's rights are also subject to death threats or worse. An activist named Manuel García de la Cruz was tortured and killed in 2002. The likely reason is that he worked for an indigenous-rights group.

Sister Dianna Ortiz, an American nun, was kidnapped by Guatemalan soldiers in 1989. In a secret prison, they raped and tortured her. Then they dropped her into an open pit of dead bodies before finally releasing her. Why did she receive this treatment? A likely reason was that she had been teaching Mayan children to read.

Rigoberta Menchú Tum organized a resistance movement against the killing of the Mayan people in Guatemala. In 1992, she was awarded the Nobel Peace Prize.

Amnesty International continues to support the work of people who call the world's attention to these crimes. One notable spokesperson is Rigoberta Menchú Tum. She is a Mayan whose family was killed in the Guatemalan fighting. Tum fled to Mexico for her life. There she organized peaceful resistance movements and became a strong voice for indigenous rights. Despite losing loved ones to violence, Tum practiced peaceful means of opposition.

Several years later, with Amnesty International's support, Tum charged four Guatemalan generals with war crimes. She insisted they stand trial and be brought to justice. Her actions helped lay the groundwork for a new campaign for international justice.

The Beginnings

Amnesty International began in November 1960. A British lawyer sat in the London subway train reading a newspaper. A small headline caught his attention. When he read the first words, he could hardly believe his eyes. But as Peter Benenson continued to read, his disbelief turned to anger and then to rage.

What inflamed him so? He read about two college students in Portugal who had just been sentenced to seven years in prison. Why? In a Lisbon bar, they had lifted their glasses in a toast to freedom.

A dictator ran Portugal at that time. He did not allow freedom of expression or other liberties. Few people dared to voice their opinions or criticize his government. If they did, they could be arrested.

This injustice had a powerful effect on Benenson. Just the year before, he had organized a group of lawyers to support human rights. They used the Universal Declaration of Human Rights as their guide. Now they had a chance to take action!

The group sent letters of protest to the Portuguese government. They respectfully asked it to release the two students. Before long, the group heard about similar cases in other countries. They started writing letters on behalf of other prisoners of conscience, too. Still, it was a lot to take on. To fight the world's injustices would require more than just a handful of people.

Benenson decided to write a newspaper article. "The Forgotten Prisoners" was published in London's *The Observer* on May 28, 1961. The article told of nine prisoners of conscience held in different countries. It urged readers to pressure those governments to release them in a mass effort called "Appeal for Amnesty" that would run for one year.

The response was immediate. The article

"The Forgotten Prisoners"

"Open your newspaper any day of the week and you will find a report from somewhere in the world of someone being imprisoned, tortured or executed because his opinions or religion are unacceptable to his government. There are several million such people in prison—by no means all of them behind the Iron and Bamboo Curtains—and their numbers are growing. The newspaper reader feels a sickening sense of impotence. Yet if these feelings of disgust all over the world could be united into common action, something effective could be done."

— The opening paragraph of Peter Benenson's article, "The Forgotten Prisoners," published in *The Observer*, 1961

Burmese residents of Japan march in a 2002 protest against the imprisonment of Aung San Suu Kyi, a prisoner of conscience who urges democracy for her homeland of Myanmar.

was reprinted in newspapers in the United States, Europe, and Asia. People flooded the governments with letters. They sent money and offers of help to Benenson. They wanted to know what they could do in their own countries.

The original plan called for people to "adopt" prisoners of conscience. Besides writing the governments, people could also write to the prisoners and their families, unless writing to a prisoner might put him or her in danger. It soon became clear that this could take longer than a year. More and more cases were being added. Benenson and his partners would have to help people start their own local groups.

Each group, Benenson said, should focus on three different cases. One case would involve a prisoner of conscience somewhere in the "First World." This included the United States and Western Europe. Another case should involve a prisoner of conscience in the "Second World." This included the Soviet Union and Eastern Europe. The third case should involve a prisoner in the "Third World." This included Latin America, Asia, Africa, and the Middle East.

Benenson believed that focusing on all types of government equally would help the organization remain impartial. This was vital in gaining people's trust.

Peter Benenson, Founder of Amnesty International

Peter Benenson was born in England in 1921. From an early age, he spoke up for what he believed. As a child in boarding school, he complained about the cafeteria's food. The school wrote his mother about his "revolutionary tendencies." When he was sixteen, he started a campaign to help orphans from the Spanish Civil War. He even "adopted" an orphan himself by sending financial support. His next student campaign, during World War II, succeeded in getting two young Jews out of Nazi Germany. Then he joined the British Army.

After the war, Benenson became a lawyer. International justice quickly became his focus. He helped defend people he felt were being bullied by those in power. He observed court trials in Spain, Cyprus, South Africa, and other countries. He organized other lawyers to promote justice for unfairly accused people.

With the formation of Amnesty International in 1961, Benenson worked harder than ever. He led research missions abroad to find out the truth about prisoners of conscience and others who had "disappeared." One time he even disguised himself so he could get into a certain country.

In 2001, Benenson remarked, "Forty years on, Amnesty International has secured many victories. . . . But the challenges are still great. Torture is banned, but in two-thirds of the world's countries it is still being committed in secret. Too many governments still allow wrongful imprisonment, murder or 'disappearance' to be carried out by their officials with impunity. Those who today still feel a sense of impotence can do something: they can support Amnesty International. They can help it to stand up for freedom and justice."

The Amnesty International Logo

The Amnesty International logo, or symbol, is a candle surrounded by barbed wire. In spite of the barbed wire, the candle flame burns brightly.

In celebrating Amnesty International's fortieth anniversary, Peter Benenson recalled, "Once the concentration camps and the

hellholes of the world were in darkness. Now they are lit by the light of the Amnesty candle, the candle in barbed wire. When I first lit the Amnesty candle, I had in mind the old Chinese proverb: 'Better light a candle than curse the darkness.'"

Today the candle and barbed wire represent hope to all who know of the efforts of Amnesty International.

Guided by these principles, Appeal for Amnesty grew rapidly. In 1962, it changed its name to better fit its larger scope. It became Amnesty International, a permanent movement to defend human rights.

Early Successes and Opposition

By the end of the organization's first year, twelve countries gave partial or complete amnesty to prisoners of conscience. These included Portugal, South Korea, Iraq, and Sudan. Several other governments definitely appeared to be aware of Amnesty International's efforts but did not actually grant amnesty to the prisoners.

By the end of 1964, the organization had brought about the release of 329 adopted prisoners of conscience. Among them was a Russian archbishop who had been imprisoned in Siberia for eighteen years.

Amnesty International celebrated its tenth year in 1971. By then, it had a thousand volunteer groups in twenty-eight countries. Brazil was a major focus of action. The Brazilian government said it had put five hundred "terrorists" in prison. AI researchers estimated closer to twelve thousand. The Soviet Union also came under examination because political prisoners were held in mental hospitals and harshly treated.

Amnesty International had its share of **controversy** as well. In 1964, founders disagreed over the case of a courageous South African leader. For daring to speak up against an unjust government, he was sentenced to life in prison. Everyone recognized the importance of his cause. However, he believed that violence was needed, if only as a last resort, to fight injustice. Because it opposed the use of violence, Amnesty International did not adopt him as a prisoner of conscience.

Twenty-six years later, he was finally released from prison. In 1993, he won the Nobel Peace Prize. In 1994, he was elected president of South Africa. His name is Nelson Mandela.

Over the years, not everyone agreed with all of Amnesty International's policies. Benenson himself did not approve of all decisions. At times he was angry when certain people were not adopted as prisoners of conscience. He also grew concerned when people accused the organization of "looking the other way" when it came to British violations of human rights. For this and other reasons, he insisted the organization must always strive to be impartial.

Nelson Mandela, seen here in 1994 voting for the first time, spent twenty-six years in prison. Amnesty International did not support him as a prisoner of conscience.

Of course, government officials responsible for human-rights abuses did not welcome Amnesty International's efforts. Their opposition took several forms. Many denied that violations had ever taken place. Some called the reports lies and **propaganda**. Violence sometimes occurred. The organization's London headquarters was attacked after publication of a report on South African security forces.

Most troubling were threats of **retaliation** as a result of the campaigns. Sometimes violent acts of revenge were carried out against prisoners of conscience, their families, or their defenders. Over the years, this problem of retaliation has not gone away. Instead, it has grown.

In Guatemala, for example, Amnesty International is very concerned about the safety of the legal community. Judges, lawyers, and others who investigate abuses from the civil war commonly receive death threats. In connection with just one case, a number of witnesses were recently killed. Dozens more were forced to flee the country with their families. Teachers, nuns, social workers, and activists have been silenced through murder or "disappearances." Meanwhile, those responsible for the crimes remain unpunished.

In response to problems like this, Amnesty International is promoting the International Justice campaign. A major goal of the campaign has been the creation of an International Criminal Court (ICC). This is a permanent world court with independent judges where the world can put war criminals and other abusers of human rights on trial. It differs from the United Nations' International Court of Justice, which is based in the Netherlands and has general responsibility for settling legal disputes between nations. Instead, the ICC, which began its work in 2003, holds individuals—even heads of state—accountable for their crimes against others. The accused would no longer be shielded by their own legal systems. If found guilty, they would personally have to make amends to victims of the crimes.

Children in Russia

For years, Anatoly lived on the streets. Although it was hard at first, he was a quick learner. He prided himself on his survival skills.

Finally, however, the police caught up with him. They grabbed him, went through his pockets, and seized a cigarette lighter. "Thief!" they announced. They handcuffed him and shoved him into the back of a truck packed with other recent arrests. At the police station, they questioned Anatoly and even beat him. But it could have been worse, he thought. Eventually, they charged him with a crime and put him in a crowded detention cell to await a trial. The wait took eleven months.

The day of the trial arrived. Anatoly hoped his luck was returning.

Surely his months in detention would count for something. Hadn't he already served enough time?

The court announced its decision: Anatoly was guilty of theft, a serious crime. For this he must serve a prison sentence of five years. Once more, Anatoly tried to tell himself that things could have been worse. But now he had trouble believing it. Five years is a long time for a fifteen-year-old boy.

Unfortunately, Anatoly's story is all too common in Russia. Formerly the core of the Soviet Union, Russia became independent in 1991, along with four-

A boy in Russia begs on a busy street. The sign says, "Help me. I want to eat."

teen other republics. Since then, it has gone through tremendous political and social changes. Adjusting to change is not easy. Although people in Russia have more freedoms than before, poverty and unemployment are widespread. This has strained even the prison system.

Human-rights groups report that in 2002, the number of Russians in jail decreased from one million to about 950,000. However, tens of thousands of Russian prisoners are under the age of eighteen. Amnesty International observers have disturbing information about the cruel treatment these children face. It is part of a pattern of human-rights abuse that persists despite recent reforms.

Youngsters like Anatoly are routinely arrested for minor crimes. In police custody, they go through interrogation, or persistent questioning. There is no requirement that a child's parents or family members be there. Lawyers who could represent the children's interests are not there, either. The police, in order to keep their jobs, try to get as many confessions of guilt as possible, using beatings, rapes, and other forms of torture.

Children are then moved to detention centers to wait for their trials. In some cases, this can take four years or longer. Some children are held in juvenile colonies. Others, though, are put in regular prisons with adults. Because of their youth, children are easy targets of violence from adult prisoners and guards.

Inside the prisons, overcrowding and disease are a way of life. Jails built to hold two hundred thousand inmates are crammed with three hundred thousand. Buildings are old and filthy with inadequate plumbing. Rats and other pests outnumber the prisoners. Tuberculosis, a contagious disease that affects the lungs, is widespread.

Amnesty International is coordinating a massive effort to persuade Russia to correct this situation. For example, people can sign a petition and send it to the Russian president, Vladimir Putin. The petition asks Russia to honor treaties, or agreements it signed with other nations, that include promises to respect the rights of women, children, and ethnic minorities as well as promises not to use torture or cruel punishment.

The petition asks Russia to train police in how to treat children in their custody. It asks that police avoid arresting children except as a last resort. Amnesty International will present the signed petition to President Putin.

Russian children are thrown into crowded prison cells with adults with no measures to keep them safe.

Working for Human Rights

Over the years, Amnesty International has developed many methods to achieve its goals, although the petition is an important one. If there is one common element in all of Amnesty's successful campaigns, perhaps it is the power of numbers. It may be easy to ignore one voice of conscience, but it is very difficult to ignore a million.

Peter Benenson noted during the organization's fortieth anniversary, "I became aware that lawyers themselves were not able sufficiently to influence the course of justice in undemocratic countries. It was necessary to think of a larger group which harnessed the enthusiasm of people all over the world who were anxious to see a wider respect for human rights."

Fortunately, Benenson and his partners had a flair for publicity. This helped spread the word about the organization in its early days. Reporters and TV news crews in Britain and elsewhere ran stories. Some even tracked down the names of prisoners of conscience in their own countries. Then they passed the details on to Benenson and the others so they could take action. It helped that Amnesty International was becoming known as an independent and impartial organization.

In the beginning, Amnesty International accepted only individual cases. With each successful release of a prisoner of conscience, its reputation grew. Other organizations, such as the United Nations, took notice. Amnesty International realized it could be more effective by working with established groups like these in addition to working directly with the public.

In 1964, the United Nations gave consultative status to Amnesty International. This meant that the UN agreed to share its resources with the new organization for the sake of their common goals. The resources included office space, research documents, and staff.

As Amnesty International matured, it developed working relationships with other such organizations as well. Gradually, it expanded its scope beyond individual cases. In 1972, the organization launched its first

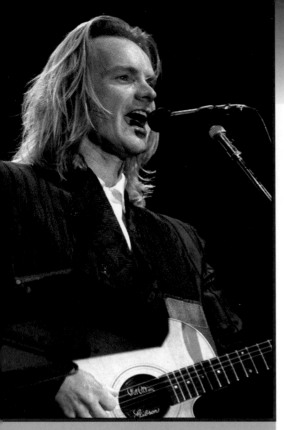

A performance by British singer-songwriter Sting launched an Amnesty International global rock tour for human rights in 1988.

worldwide campaign. This campaign was devoted to the overall goal of banning the use of torture everywhere.

For this type of effort, a huge amount of fieldwork is required. First, Amnesty International sends research teams to the area or areas in question. They investigate cases, collect facts, and observe court trials. They interview prisoners and victims, their families, and other human-rights workers in the area.

Amnesty International may coordinate legal aid for cases as part of the campaign to ensure that people are fairly represented in court. It may also help appeal decisions that are unfavorable, such as in the case of Nigerian mother Amina Lawal.

Financial assistance may also be given. The organization withdraws money from a fund created in 1962. Money from this fund helps prisoners of conscience and their families who need it most. In 2001, about $170,000 was used to aid several families and to help torture victims get medical treatment.

Perhaps the most important service Amnesty International provides is public education. It seeks to heighten public awareness of human rights with a variety of activities. Famous entertainers donate their talents to films, shows, and other events to raise money. Top rock stars such as Sting, U2, and Bruce Springsteen have held huge charity concerts covered by the media. Membership in Amnesty International grows as a result of these events. For example, after the 1988 "Human Rights Now!" concert world tour, membership rose dramatically in Argentina, Brazil, Greece, India, and several other countries.

The organization also trains leaders of local volunteer groups. It offers guidance on letter-writing campaigns, demonstrations, fund-raisers, and other programs. In addition, a number of books, videos, and publications inform people about Amnesty International. Many of these can be ordered from the Amnesty International web site.

Structure of the Organization

Amnesty International is a grassroots organization. That means that ordinary citizens all over the world do the bulk of its work. These people are volunteers. They give their time freely because they believe in the goals of Amnesty International.

Volunteers can work by themselves or in groups. Groups are formed in neighborhoods, communities, churches, schools, youth centers, and college campuses. Often one group associates with others to form a regional network. A network may include groups in different cities or countries. Together they work toward a common goal. According to its 2002 Annual Report, Amnesty International has more than 7,800 local groups around the world.

Who coordinates all the local groups in a country? That work is handled by a national section, or office. For example, all groups in France report to the French national section. All groups in Ireland report to the Irish national

A researcher from Amnesty International discusses the experiences of a boy forced to serve as a soldier in Sierra Leone in 2000.

section. There are currently fifty-six national sections. An International Council coordinates the work of the national sections, and representatives from each national section take part. The Council meets every two years. It makes major decisions to guide the organization and its activities. It can review rules and vote to change them if necessary.

The Council also elects eight members to an International Executive Committee (IEC), and the International Secretariat elects one from among its members. The IEC carries out the Council's decisions. It also appoints a secretary-general who heads both the International Council and the International Secretariat.

The International Secretariat is the research arm of the organization, based in the London headquarters. It has more than three hundred paid staff and many volunteers. These people collect information from all over the world, using newspaper and magazine articles, reports from rights activists, and letters from prisoners of conscience. They go on research

AI's Secretary-General

Irene Khan, born in Bangladesh, is the current secretary-general of Amnesty International. She was appointed in August 2001 to lead the organization. She is the first woman, first Asian, and first Muslim to hold this position.

Ms. Khan studied international law and has worked for years to protect the rights of refugees. Early in her career, she joined the United Nations High Commission for Refugees. There she held several leadership positions and developed a number of programs. She also participated in emergency operations to help people displaced by war. Since joining Amnesty International, Ms. Khan has traveled widely to bring the world's attention to human rights for all.

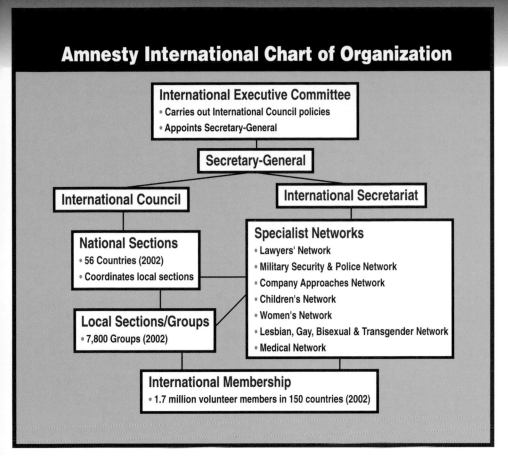

Amnesty International Chart of Organization

International Executive Committee
- Carries out International Council policies
- Appoints Secretary-General

Secretary-General

International Council

International Secretariat

National Sections
- 56 Countries (2002)
- Coordinates local sections

Specialist Networks
- Lawyers' Network
- Military Security & Police Network
- Company Approaches Network
- Children's Network
- Women's Network
- Lesbian, Gay, Bisexual & Transgender Network
- Medical Network

Local Sections/Groups
- 7,800 Groups (2002)

International Membership
- 1.7 million volunteer members in 150 countries (2002)

missions to the countries in question. After firsthand investigation, they write reports and make recommendations. Amnesty International publishes these reports and recommendations. Volunteer networks, groups, and members then get the information they need to take action.

A Refugee in Lebanon

Like many in his home country of Sudan, a young man named Ibrahim feared for his life. Civil war and famine had crippled his African nation as long as he could remember. In 1999, Ibrahim left in search of a safer life.

Since the mid-1980s, more than four million Sudanese have fled their homeland to escape violence and starvation. They have gone to nearby countries looking for a place that will accept them. At the very least, they want to be protected until they can find somewhere else to settle.

Ibrahim made his way north to Lebanon, in the Middle East, where he

The Nobel Peace Prize

The Nobel Peace Prize recognizes outstanding efforts to promote brotherhood and cooperation among nations while reducing violent conflicts. In 1977, Amnesty International received the Nobel Peace Prize for its ongoing work to secure freedom, justice, and peace for citizens all over the world. The prize was accepted on behalf of Amnesty International by one of its International Executive Committee members, a former prisoner of conscience from Turkey named Mumtaz Soysal. In his acceptance speech, he said, "Peace is not to be measured by the absence of conventional war, but constructed upon foundations of justice. Where there is injustice, there is the seed of conflict. Where human rights are violated, there are threats to peace."

Over the years, the work of many Nobel Peace Prize recipients has intersected that of Amnesty International. Following are the names of just a few who have lent their support to Amnesty International campaigns and/or been helped by such campaigns.

- Seán MacBride, Ireland (1974), for his leadership of many human-rights organizations, including Amnesty International
- Betty Williams, United Kingdom (1976), for founding the Northern Ireland Peace Movement
- Lech Walesa, Poland (1983), for leadership of the Solidarity movement dedicated to workers' right to organize
- Desmond Tutu, South Africa (1984), for peaceful work to end racist apartheid
- Oscar Arias Sanchez, Costa Rica (1987), for helping to negotiate peace in Central America

asked for **asylum,** or protection. He wanted Lebanese authorities to let him stay rather than send him back, or **deport** him. He knew the military government in Sudan would punish him for leaving. He also applied for refugee status at a United Nations office. As an official refugee, he would be safe from deportation. He was also supposed to be safe while his application was being considered. During this waiting period, Ibrahim stayed in the Lebanese capital of Beirut. Unfortunately,

- The 14th Dalai Lama, Tibet (1989), for his international human-rights work, global environmentalism, and nonviolent struggle to liberate his people from China
- Aung San Suu Kyi, Myanmar (1991), for her nonviolent struggle for democracy and human rights
- Rigoberta Menchú Tum, Guatemala (1992), for her work in support of social justice and respect for the rights of indigenous people
- Jody Williams, United States (1997), for coordinating a campaign to ban and clear land mines from several continents

American Jody Williams, with Korean soldiers, inspected the terrain for land mines in the DMZ (Demilitarized Zone) between North and South Korea.

in 2001, Lebanese police arrested a group of people they accused of being "illegal immigrants." Ibrahim was one of the people in the crowd. As he tried to escape over a wall, a police officer shot the refugee, killing him.

Amnesty International immediately wrote Lebanon for an explanation. Authorities said that Ibrahim had resisted arrest—he had hit the hand of the officer holding the gun. This caused the gun to fire and fatally wound him. However, other witnesses at the scene say he was actually shot in

Families seeking safety from war may find themselves living for many years in refugee camps, such as this one in Lebanon.

the back from a short distance.

In 1951, a United Nations treaty laid out specific rights for refugees. Many nations signed the treaty and agreed to honor refugee rights. Lebanon did not sign it, but Amnesty International insists that Lebanon should follow international law that protects refugees. Mistreatment of refugees is a growing concern. This is true not only in Lebanon but in many other countries as well. Even the United States is under investigation for mistreating refugees. The situation has grown worse since terrorists attacked New York and Washington, D.C., on September 11, 2001.

Amnesty International charges that many governments use fear of terrorism as an excuse to restrict human rights. For example, people suspected of being terrorists can be put on trial in a special military court. This involves "wartime" or emergency rules that do not follow human-rights law. People might be arrested and held without specific explanations. Furthermore, refugees trying to survive in a new land may become targets of **racism**, or the belief that certain races are better than others. It is the basis of hate crimes against people who simply look different or speak a different language.

Almost certainly, racism was one factor that led to the death of Ibrahim in Lebanon.

Campaigns and Urgent Actions

Today, much of Amnesty International's work concerns human-rights violations that have gone on for years. Often these involve large groups of people and similar patterns of abuse across various countries.

It takes patience and persistence to get positive results. Not everyone agrees with the organization's methods or cooperates with its efforts. Most would admit, however, that human rights are violated on every continent. And most would agree that Amnesty International has called the world's attention to the importance of respecting human rights.

Toward that end, one of its current campaigns is Human Rights Education. This campaign will probably continue indefinitely. Amnesty takes the view that all the organization's activities consist of educating the public and governments in human rights. The Human Rights Education campaign focuses specifically on educating the next generation of human-rights defenders. It is designed for children, youth, and those who care about them. The campaign includes children from kindergarten through grade twelve, college students, parents, teachers, and other dedicated adults.

For teachers and activists, the organization offers a Human Rights Educators' Network. People in the network make presentations at school assemblies, university events, conferences, and exhibits. They help prepare

Human-rights education begins with even the very youngest children. This child participated in an educational activity in New Zealand in 2001.

Some Current Campaigns

The following Amnesty International campaigns take positions on ongoing human-rights issues.
- Russia: Justice for Everybody. Despite recent reforms, human-rights abuse continues.
- Stop Torture. Torture is still used throughout the world against prisoners, including women and children.
- The Death Penalty. This ultimate punishment violates the right to life.
- Colombia: Breaking Down the Wall of Silence. Innocent civilians are drawn into the ongoing conflict between the government and rebel forces.
- Economic Relations and Human Rights. Businesses must be responsible for the human-rights impacts of their activities.
- Child Soldiers. More than three hundred thousand children under eighteen are fighting in conflicts around the globe, with hundreds of thousands more enlisted in armed forces — many against their will.
- Justice, Not Revenge. In the wake of the September 11, 2001, attacks and the U.S. response against terrorism, real security can be achieved only by respecting everyone's human rights.
- Guatemala: The Lethal Legacy of Impunity. Guatemala's legal community has failed to bring war criminals and human-rights abusers to justice.

information and may act as faculty advisors for AI student groups.

The network also sponsors many global projects. One of the most successful is in the Philippines. There, many programs teach students how to raise public awareness about human rights. In the Netherlands, human-rights education is required for all police academy graduates. In the South American country of Guyana, a teacher-training project is underway.

Of course, education begins in the home. Amnesty International offers a variety of activities and resources for children and parents. They can do letter writing and holiday card campaigns together. They can read books, magazines, and newsletters together. They can watch videotapes or use an interactive CD-ROM program.

Urgent Actions

Campaigns are designed to last a while, but what does Amnesty International do in more urgent cases? What about prisoners of conscience who are at immediate risk of torture or disappearance?

The surprise arrest of Luiz Rossi, a Brazilian college professor, was such a case. One night in February 1973, police surrounded his house and quickly took him into custody. No explanation was given for the arrest. Rossi feared the worst. A military **dictatorship** was in charge at the time. It was known that many prisoners were tortured.

Luckily, Rossi's wife managed to pass a secret note to a neighbor. Eventually her note reached Amnesty International headquarters. The organization responded immediately with a new strategy called an Urgent Action. It immediately alerted volunteer members about the arrest. It told them that Brazilian police would not let Rossi talk with his family or lawyers. Above all, the urgency of the case was emphasized. Rossi must be released as soon as possible because he faced torture or worse.

Soon, letters poured in to the Brazilian government. The police were surprised. They had not expected anyone to even know about the arrest, much less send letters. They could hardly believe that strangers halfway around the globe would care about one man's fate. Seven months later, Rossi was freed. He and his wife credited the prompt response of Amnesty International and its volunteers as a major factor in his release.

Today, Urgent Actions still work in much the same way. When Amnesty International researchers in London learn of an urgent case, they put together a fact

Amnesty International's first Urgent Action was to protect Professor Luiz Rossi of Brazil in 1973. He later said, "I knew that my case had become public; I knew they could no longer kill me. Then the pressure on me decreased and conditions improved."

33

sheet. This contains details about the prisoner of conscience. It includes suggestions about whom to write and what to say.

The information is then quickly distributed to an Urgent Action Network. This consists of members who have pledged to help. These members write or fax the governments involved. They also urge people they know to do the same.

Children can take part in these efforts as well, along with parents or teachers. In fact, a Junior Urgent Action Network has been created for this very purpose. The first Junior Urgent Action took place in 1993. The immediate goal was to help children in the South American country of Colombia. Soldiers were threatening their families. Many people were forced to leave their homes. However, the situation improved after an immediate letter-writing campaign by the Junior Urgent Action Network. Children played a big role in this effort.

Other Junior Urgent Actions followed. Usually, these involved cases of children suffering human-rights abuses. So far, efforts have been made on behalf of young people in fifty countries.

Protesting Working Conditions in China

Workers in the silk factories were fed up. Despite bosses' promises, their workplaces were getting worse, not better. Chemical fumes made them ill. There was little or no ventilation. Safety equipment was scarce, so accidents were common. Injured and sick employees had to pay doctors out of their own pockets, not from company funds.

Many employees had to work overtime, too. Usually they received no extra pay. They were also angry about a new factory rule that said they could not get married or have children. The bosses thought no one would dare complain. After more than five million workers in China lost their jobs in 1999, the bosses figured people were lucky to have jobs at all. The workers had many things to protest, but even protest was not allowed. Independent workers' **unions** were illegal in China.

Chinese workers have been imprisoned for protesting against inadequate working conditions and poor pay. These women paint toys in a crowded factory in Zhuhai in southern China.

Finally, the workers demonstrated. It started as a peaceful protest. Soon, police arrived. Dozens of people were injured. Even more were arrested. Some individuals seen as "protest leaders" were put in prison. The authorities did not say when they would be released.

More than one billion people live within China's borders. For the past twenty years, the Chinese government has tried to put the economy on a more equal footing with other countries. Some things have changed in Chinese society, but political freedoms are still scarce.

Amnesty International wants the human-rights situation to improve in China. It asks the government to respect freedom of assembly and freedom of expression. Citizens should be allowed to meet privately and voice their opinions without fear of being jailed. Workers' dignity should

In a march to the Government House in Hong Kong in 2002, Chinese protesters carried a banner that said, "Stop exploiting workers." For many years, Chinese people had been afraid to protest.

be respected. People should not have to work under harsh conditions. They should be allowed to form unions and have nonviolent protests.

In China, as in many other countries, the legal and prison system is a major concern. Citizens can be arrested even if they have not committed crimes. The homeless, mentally ill, and disabled may be rounded up and taken to jail. Often, they are not even charged with actual crimes. One million Chinese are detained this way every year.

Another arrest method is called "re-education through labor." Individuals who commit minor crimes are never charged or put on trial. Instead, they automatically receive sentences of one to four years in work camps, where conditions are very harsh.

The death penalty in China is a special concern. In April 2001, the Chinese government intensified its ongoing anticrime program with the "Strike Hard" campaign. Thousands of people were arrested for such crimes as bribery of officials, and more than four thousand death sentences were handed out in 2001. Of these, more than half the people were executed the same year.

Success Stories

Without a doubt, much remains to be done on behalf of human rights. Yet progress is made and positive outcomes do result. Amnesty International rarely claims direct credit when prisoners of conscience are released. But certainly its hard work—together with volunteer efforts and other factors—has a significant impact.

One example is the case of two Mexican peasants who were arrested in 1999. Their only "crime" had been to work with environmental groups. They wanted to keep local forests from being logged too heavily. The two men were tortured, jailed on false charges, and sentenced to prison.

Amnesty International coordinated a letter-writing campaign to free the two men. In November 2001, Mexican President Vicente Fox, who had been elected after the arrests, released them. A human-rights worker observed, "Their release demonstrates that international pressure is mightier than the political will of those in power."

Meanwhile, another Mexican citizen had spent more than eight years in jail. He was General José Gallardo, a well-known leader for human rights. Soldiers had arrested him in 1993 for speaking out against the military's human-rights violations. In 1994, Amnesty International members started working for Gallardo's release. It took a long time, but President Fox freed Gallardo in February 2002.

Punishing Songwriters in Tibet

Halfway around the world, Chinese police arrested a Tibetan Buddhist nun named Ngawang Sangdrol. It was 1992, and she was only fifteen at the time. She and other nuns were accused of antigovernment activities and imprisoned. In prison, she and others secretly wrote and recorded songs about Tibet, their homeland, which the Chinese had invaded decades before. Prison officials discovered the songs and punished the nuns. Sangdrol was beaten, and her prison term was extended to 2011.

Amnesty International volunteers took on her case. They kept up their protests for many years. In October 2002, Sangdrol was released ahead of

Activists from student groups protest the imprisonment of Tibetan nuns in front of the Chinese Consulate in New York City in 2002. Such protests, which gain public attention, are an important part of Amnesty International's activities.

time for good behavior. In all, she served ten years before being released.

Long prison terms are common for Tibetans jailed for their religious or political beliefs. A music scholar was sentenced to eighteen years. A former schoolteacher spent nearly forty years in prison. These men had publicly protested against China's takeover of Tibet. After extended efforts by Amnesty International, they were released in 2002. In thanking the organization, the scholar urged members to continue working for the release of other Tibetan prisoners of conscience.

Acknowledging Amnesty's Help

Amnesty International receives grateful letters from many individuals and families. For example, a human-rights group from the African country of Kenya found Amnesty International's help invaluable. They had been arrested in 2001 on charges of "unlawful assembly" just for holding an independence celebration. After letters and faxes flooded government offices for six days, the authorities decided to let the group go. The group said the protest letters were a key factor in their release.

Likewise, in 1997, a human-rights activist in Mexico thanked Amnesty International members for their letters and faxes to government agencies on his behalf. "They have assured us that we are not alone and they have shown the government that an entire international network is aware of anything that might happen to us and is ready to respond."

Alpha Condé, a leader in the African nation of Guinea, also expressed thanks to Amnesty International. In 1998, he led an independent political party and ran for president, but the elections were not run fairly by the government. Riots broke out. Many opposition leaders, including Condé, questioned the voting results. The next day, he was arrested. So were more than sixty members of his political party. Many later said they were tortured while in police custody. In the meantime, Amnesty International worked for Condé's release. He got it in May 2001, along with a presidential pardon. "Thanks to the support of Amnesty International members, I never felt alone," he wrote.

Just knowing that others are aware of their situation can lift prisoners' spirits. This was true of four women in the Middle Eastern country of Kuwait. In 1991, the courts falsely convicted them of helping enemy forces during the Persian Gulf War. Amnesty International adopted the women as prisoners of conscience. After ten years in jail, they were finally pardoned and released. One woman gratefully acknowledged Amnesty International's ongoing efforts.

A journalist from Tajikistan (formerly part of the Soviet Union) said Amnesty International made a big difference in his case. He had left Tajikistan only to be detained by Russian authorities. But after a network of volunteers pressured the Russian government, he was released. He said Amnesty International's efforts helped keep prisoners like him from being lost or forgotten.

Nearby, a political prisoner in Uzbekistan (another former Soviet republic) was waiting to be executed. He never knew which day would be his last. His situation improved after Amnesty International got involved. The Supreme Court of Uzbekistan reduced his sentence to fifteen years in prison. His sister wrote Amnesty International: "You helped to preserve my brother's life. . . . We are eternally indebted to you because life has no price."

In Opposition to Amnesty International

"All the lackeys of satanic powers like Amnesty International . . . are trying to suffocate the Islamic republic . . ."
Ayatollah Khomeini, Iran, 1982

Indeed, some things cannot be measured. A woman named Sara Méndez was separated from her infant son. It was twenty-five years before she saw him again. Méndez and her husband were refugees from Uruguay in South America. Fearing the Uruguayan military government, they fled to Argentina in 1976. They lived there under false names to hide their identities; however, they were discovered. Less than a month after Méndez gave birth to a son, soldiers came to arrest her. They separated her from her baby, then flew her back to Uruguay. She remained in prison for five years and was cruelly treated.

Upon her release, she started searching for her son. Local human-rights groups assisted her. They made progress, but it was slow. In July 2001, Amnesty International urged Uruguay to cooperate with all such searches for "disappeared" persons. The organization made a special appeal for Sara Méndez. Hadn't she waited long enough?

Less than a year later, a judge brought good news. The boy, who was now a man, had been located! Adopted by a family in Argentina, he had been living with them all this time. Finally, Méndez and her twenty-five-year-old son were reunited.

What Individuals Can Do

Anyone who wants to help can take part in the activities of Amnesty International. There are many things that people of all ages can do. One suggestion is to find out whether there is an Amnesty International group in the area by looking through a phone book or newspaper. If there is a local group, when and where does it hold its meetings? What activities are planned? Perhaps a parent or older brother or sister can accompany a young person to the meeting. An interested person should ask questions. Is the group working on a project in which young people can take part? Perhaps someone from the group would be willing to talk at school and share why he or she joined Amnesty International.

In the days before Operation Iraqi Freedom began in 2003, Amnesty International members held a number of vigils protesting against the war. This silent vigil was held in Parliament Square in London.

A teacher, coach, or counselor may want to get involved. For example, some teachers have organized letter-writing projects for their classes. The Junior Urgent Action Network is a good starting point. Monthly materials are available from AI USA (Children's Edition Urgent Actions), AI Canada (Lifesavers), and AI UK (Junior Urgent Actions). One of the Junior Network's activities is a "Holiday Card Action," which usually takes place at the end of the year. Students are asked to make and send cheerful nonreligious cards to three prisoners of conscience. Complete details are given about whom to write to and where to send the cards.

Other students in different cities or countries may be doing similar projects. Sometimes teachers can arrange for their students to become pen pals with other students who live far away.

Amnesty International does not accept money from governments. To do its work, it must rely entirely on donations from the public. Young people can help by contributing money (with parental permission) or time. For example, newsletters or flyers can be folded at meetings.

Education is a big part of this organization. Local groups often sponsor guest speakers, walk-a-thons, or other events. Friends and neighbors might like to find out about these events and participate, too.

Of course, Amnesty International always appreciates its success stories being shared with other people. This does not have to be limited to class-mates. Stories can be shared with soccer team members, scouting groups, and after-school clubs.

Individuals can watch videos and read books to learn more about human-rights issues. They can subscribe to Amnesty International magazines or sign up to receive free e-mail bulletins. They can listen to tapes or CDs from Amnesty International concert tours. Music superstars such as Peter Gabriel and Paul McCartney often give interviews to share reasons why they help promote Amnesty International ideas.

Finally, a recommendation given by many people who are involved in Amnesty International or other human-rights organizations is to be open

A Message of Hope: "Imagine" Campaign 2003

Music is universal. It can reach across borders and into hearts. No matter what languages people speak, the power of a simple melody can bring them together.

With that in mind, Amnesty International has started a new campaign. It is based on John Lennon's song, "Imagine." This song is known the world over for its message of peace and brotherhood. It says, "Imagine all the people sharing all the world." With the help of this song, Amnesty International wants to educate more people than ever before about human rights.

The two-year "Imagine" campaign was launched on International Human Rights Day, December 10, 2002. It included print, television, radio and internet advertisements; TV events; and school and community activities. A music video was created featuring children singing the song in South Africa, Northern Ireland, Croatia, Cambodia, Thailand, and the United States. A CD single produced by Academy-Award-winning producer Hans Zimmer (The Lion King) features a new version of "Imagine" sung by children from different countries backed by famous musicians.

The idea for the video came from Irish actor Gabriel Byrne and John Lennon's widow, Yoko Ono Lennon (above). She worked hard with Amnesty International to develop the "Imagine" campaign. "I've found that most children, even when they're five or six, know the lyrics of 'Imagine,'"she says. "By asking children of different countries to sing the song, it's a way of getting children to come together."

She also believes that each and every person can play a part in making this world a better place to live. "Every day," she says, "do something that makes your heart dance. And if your heart is so depressed that you can't dance, then do something that will make other people's hearts dance ... it could be as simple as giving a phone call. If you kept doing that for three months, you'd see an incredible change in your life.... And if your life changes, well, in the same manner, we can change the world, also."

to new experiences. This includes respecting those in the community who may look or act different. One way to learn about other cultures and customs is to visit services at a different church or synagogue, mosque or temple. It becomes clear that people are not really very different from each other; they have more in common than they realize.

All people are born with human rights. The people of Amnesty International hope to make recognition of these rights a reality for everyone.

WRITING LETTERS: A guide from Amnesty International

Amnesty International makes the following suggestions for writing a letter regarding a prisoner of conscience:

1. Always be polite. This rule is essential and invariable. Your aim is to help a prisoner, not to relieve your own feelings. Governments don't respond to abusive or condemnatory letters (however well deserved).

2. Always write your letters on the basis that the government concerned is open to reason and discussion.

3. It is important where possible to stress a country's reputation for moderation and justice, to show respect for its constitution and judicial procedures, and to demonstrate an understanding of current difficulties. This will give more scope to point out ways in which the human-rights situation can be improved.

4. Follow strictly the instructions given by Amnesty International in the case in question. For instance, if the World Wide Appeal asks you to appeal for medical treatment for a prisoner, make sure that you request this, and not a speedy trial or release, which might be appropriate in another case.

5. Never use political jargon. Don't give the impression that you are writing because you are ideologically or politically opposed to the government in question. It is far more effective to stress the fact that your concern for human rights is not politically based in any way but in keeping with basic principles of international law.

6. If appropriate, please explain who you are and what you do. This indicates that the letter is genuine and also shows that people from varying walks of life are following events in the country concerned.

7. If you have any special interest or link with the country, it is a good idea to mention this in your letter. For instance, you may have visited it or studied its history.

Above all, be brief. Sometimes one sentence will do.

Time Line

1948 United Nations General Assembly adopts the Universal Declaration of Human Rights.

1961 Peter Benenson writes newspaper article, "The Forgotten Prisoners." Group is formed under the name "Appeal for Amnesty."

1962 Appeal for Amnesty becomes Amnesty International (AI); it creates financial relief fund for prisoners of conscience.

1963 AI establishes International Secretariat and International Executive Committee to oversee all adoption group activities.

1965 AI calls for ban on capital punishment for peacetime offenses.

1967 Eighteen countries have a total of 550 AI groups.

1972 AI starts first worldwide campaign to ban torture.

1973 AI issues first full Urgent Action on behalf of Brazilian prisoner of conscience Luiz Rossi.

1975 First AI adoption group formed in Soviet Union. United Nations adopts Declaration Against Torture.

1977 AI receives Nobel Peace Prize.

1982 AI collects more than one million signatures in support of universal amnesty for all prisoners of conscience.

1985 AI broadens mission to include work on behalf of refugees.

1987 AI reports that the U.S. death penalty violates human rights.

1990 AI has seven hundred thousand members in 150 countries.

1991 On thirtieth anniversary, AI expands "prisoners of conscience" category to include people punished for their sexual orientation.

1994 AI launches worldwide campaigns on behalf of women's rights and also calls attention to "disappearances" and political killings.

1998 AI joins legal proceedings against former Chilean President Pinochet for war crimes. United Nations adopts AI's International Criminal Court campaign.

2001 AI celebrates fortieth anniversary, noting it has closed forty-five thousand of the forty-seven thousand cases it has taken on.

2003 AI promotes "Imagine" campaign of human-rights education.

Glossary

asylum protection from arrest granted by a country or other authority to refugees who have fled their own countries

controversy a situation in which people disagree or hold opposite views

deport to force a person, usually a refugee, to leave a country

dictatorship government by a ruler who takes complete control of a country and considers himself above the law

discrimination prejudicial or negative outlook, action, or treatment toward a group of people because of their color, origins, or beliefs

hostage a person who is taken captive by another and held until an action, such as paying ransom or releasing prisoners, is taken

genocide destruction of an entire group of people because of their race, color, or religion; also called ethnic cleansing

impunity freedom from punishment

indigenous born or originated in a particular place; native

intimidated frightened into agreement or submission

petition a written request made to a government or other authority that is usually signed by many people

propaganda ideas, facts, or rumors that are spread to further or damage a cause

racism a belief that race determines human abilities and traits and that some races are naturally more gifted than others

retaliation revenge

union an organization of workers with the authority to act for its members as a group

women's rights legal, social, and political rights for women equal to those of men

To Find Out More

BOOKS

Atgwa, Paul, editor. *Stand Up for Your Rights*. World Book, 1998.

Altman, Linda Jacobs. *Human Rights: Issues for a New Millennium*. Issues in Focus Series. Enslow, 2002.

Gold, Susan Dudley. *Human Rights*. Twenty-First Century Books, 1997.

Grant, R. G. *Amnesty International*. World Organizations Series. Watts, 2001.

Kuklin, Susan. *Irrepressible Spirit: Conversations With Human Rights Activists*. Philomel Books, 1996.

McGowan, Keith. *Human Rights*. Lucent Overview Series. Lucent, 2002.

Silvertone, Michael, and Charlotte Bunch. *Rigoberta Menchu: Defending Human Rights in Guatemala*. Women Changing the World Series. Feminist Press, 1999.

Williams, Mary E., editor. *Human Rights: Opposing Viewpoints*. Opposing Viewpoints Series. Greenhaven Press, 1998.

Winner, David. *Peter Benenson: Taking a Stand Against Injustice, Amnesty International*. People Who Have Helped the World Series. Gareth Stevens, 1992.

ADDRESSES AND WEB SITES

Amnesty International
International Secretariat
1 Easton Street
London WC1X 0DW, UK
www.amnesty.org

AIUSA
322 8th Avenue
New York, NY 10001
www.amnestyusa.org

Kids Can Free the Children: www.freethechildren.org/

Human Rights Watch: www.hrw.org

Index